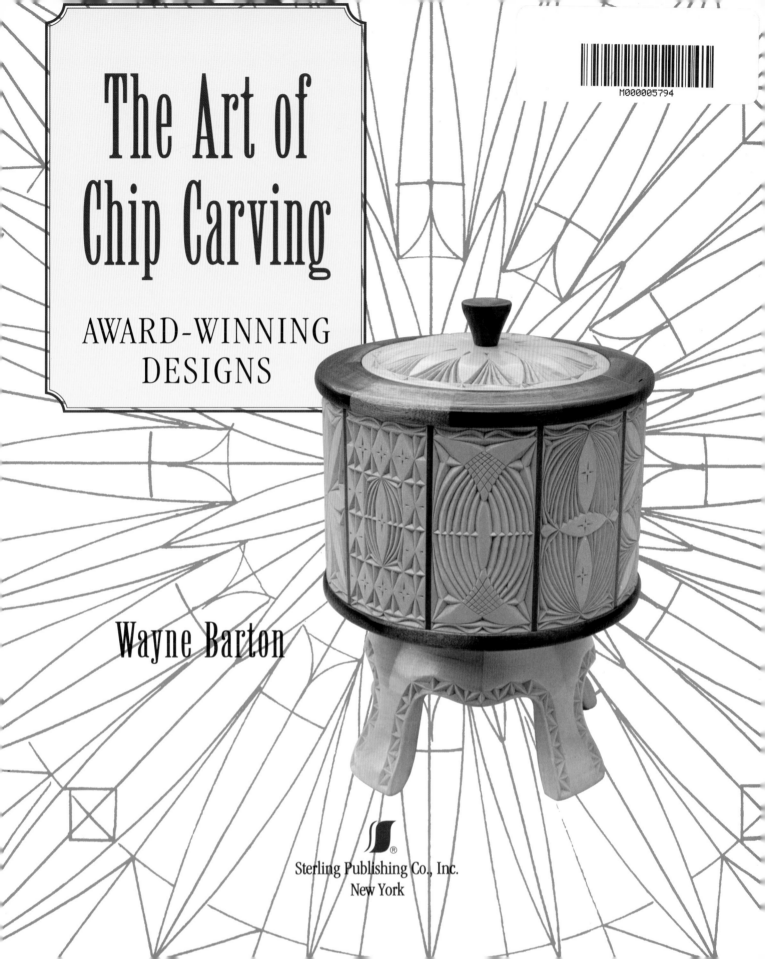

The Art of Chip Carving

AWARD-WINNING DESIGNS

Wayne Barton

Sterling Publishing Co., Inc.
New York

NOTE: All of the chip carving presented is that of the contributors, not of the author.

Front cover photo: Mickey L. Hudspeth's octagonal lidded container, in basswood and walnut.
Title page photo: Mickey L. Hudspeth's lidded bowl on stand.
p. 3: David W. Carothers' music box lid.
p. 7: Robert A. Ostmann's 10-inch basswood scoop plate.
p. 9: Mickey L. Hudspeth's coffee-table top.
p. 14: Timothy Montzka's basswood trunk lid.
p. 15: Timothy J. Balda's 14-inch rim basswood plate.
p. 18: Amorn Watanapong's tabletop.

p. 19: Barry G. McKenzie's "Sunflower" 14-inch plate.
p. 20: Donald A. Ecker's 12-inch basswood plate.
p. 21: Bert Hirt's "Eye of the Storm" rosette.
p. 23: Karen Kolisch Oquin's Hawk in flight basswood plate.
p. 24: Mickey L. Hudspeth's lidded bowl on stand.
p. 28: David W. Carothers' music box lid.
p. 30: Margaret C. Walker's 12-inch scalloped basswood plate.
p. 31: Robert E. Smith's jewelry box in basswood and walnut.
p. 32 (top): Bruce Nicholas' floral rosette on a six-inch disk.
p. 32 (bottom): Sister Mary Julius' basswood serving tray.
p. 33 (top): Robert Rymark's 12-inch bowl.
p. 33 (bottom): Rev. Jeffrey Woods' trefoil on a 4 1/2-inch disk.

Library of Congress Cataloging-in-Publication Data

Barton, Wayne.
    The art of chip carving : award-winning designs / by Wayne Barton.
        p.   cm.
    Includes index.
    ISBN 0-8069-4894-9
    1. Wood-carving. 2. Wood-carving—Patterns I. Title.
    TT199.7.B358   1998
    736'.4—dc21   97-51570
                                                        CIP

Book Design by Judy Morgan
Editing and Layout by R. Neumann

1   3   5   7   9   10   8   6   4   2

Published by Sterling Publishing Company, Inc.
387 Park Avenue South, New York, N.Y. 10016
© 1998 by Wayne Barton
Distributed in Canada by Sterling Publishing
c/o Canadian Manda Group, One Atlantic Avenue, Suite 105
Toronto, Ontario, Canada M6K 3E7
Distributed in Great Britain and Europe by Cassell PLC
Wellington House, 125 Strand, London WC2R 0BB, England
Distributed in Australia by Capricorn Link (Australia) Pty Ltd.
P.O. Box 6651, Baulkham Hills, Business Centre, NSW 2153, Australia
Printed in Hong Kong

Sterling ISBN 0-8069-4894-9

Dedication

To all of my students past, present, and future. May you discover through carving the joy, fulfillment, and friendship it has brought to me of which you have surely been a part, or will be.

Contents

Foreword

Once an activity has become a norm in our lives, there is a natural tendency to lose sight of how it came about. While chip carving has been around on a limited scale on this side of the Atlantic Ocean for years, it has only proliferated in North America over the past few years. Today chip carving is commonplace in almost all woodcarving shows, occupying its own category in most competitions.

The large-scale introduction of chip carving and the magnificent levels to which it is possible to execute this style of carving was initiated when Wayne Barton published his first article on the subject in 1984. While Wayne had been pursuing this type of carving for close to 30 years, and teaching it to those fortunate enough to cross paths with him, the carving population at large only became acquainted with the style as a result of his regular column in "Chip Chats," the magazine of the North American Woodcarvers Association, his books and videotape, other writings, and his classes.

Wayne Barton, through his superior technical and artistic abilities, coupled with his total command of how to describe and instruct others in the execution of chip carving, has singularly been responsible for the proliferation of chip carving in North America. His unselfish contributions have had an immense and pervasive effect.

When he made the decision to pursue a life in carving, Wayne went to Brienz, Switzerland, for formal study in all forms of carving under the tutelage of some of the masters who were still carving and teaching there. Upon his return to the States, he taught for a short while at the Chicago School of Woodcarving before establishing the Alpine School of Woodcarving, Ltd.

Throughout the course of his career, he didn't pay great attention to gaining personal accolades. Although he was awarded first place in any competition he entered, his focus has always been on teaching and sharing with others. He has also been recognized by the Swiss National Museum, in Zurich, which honored him by placing his work on special exhibition for 18 months. For the past four years, Wayne has also appeared on public and educational TV on the *American Woodshop* with Scott Phillips.

Besides writing three previous books, Wayne also saw the need for superior carving tools and developed the Premier chip-carving knives now in common use throughout the carving community and recognized as the best available for their superior quality. He has also developed ceramic sharpening stones and continues to create new products and objects for carvers.

Today, many carvers are happily engaged in the practice of chip carving. Some are even engaged full- or part-time professionally. With few exceptions, most instructors now passing on the knowledge of chip-carving methods, obtained their introduction and expertise in the art via exposure to Wayne and/or his classes and writings. Those who have not been trained directly by Wayne have, fortunately for us, been instructed by someone who was schooled by Wayne himself. It would be very difficult to find a finely executed example of chip carving in North America today that did not bear Wayne Barton's influence.

Especially among those of us who carve, he has had an unbelievable amount of positive influence on the lives of so many others. Anyone who has the opportunity to study with him is fortunate. Without his unswerving pursuit of and dedication to carving, chances are you never would have heard of chip carving.

David Crothers
Hatboro, PA

Preface

When I first conceived creating a book of this nature, I knew it would depend heavily upon the contributions and support of many others. It is a blessing to have had so many students who are also personal friends, willing to assist. Though some had more carvings available for photographing than others, all of their contributions were equally valuable to this effort.

This book is a pictorial celebration and testimony to the artistic spirit within us all. It shows the work of twenty-one carvers all of whom have studied with me either in class or through my books and video. (For the reader interested in learning the process of how to begin chip carving, I recommend my previous books, the 1984 *Chip Carving Techniques & Patterns*, the 1990 *Chip Carving Patterns*, and the 1994 *New & Traditional Styles of Chip Carving*, all published by Sterling Publishing Co.)

A few of the carvers presented herein carve professionally, others are enthusiasts. Their biographies reveal a cross section of age, national origin, occupation, and education demonstrating there are no boundaries to the flow of artistic expression. I would like to express my appreciation. Their willingness to share so others may learn, enjoy, and be inspired will raise the level of excellence and add to the general knowledge of chip carving.

Alphabetically they are Chuck Baker, Tim Balda, David Crothers, Don Ecker, Jeff Fleisher, Bert Hirt, Mickey Hudspeth, Sister Mary Julius, Larry Kampel, Diana Kwan, Barry McKenzie, Tim Montzka, Bruce Nicholas, Karen Kolisch Oquin, Bob Ostmann, Bob Rymark, Bob Smith, Peggy Walker, Mark Walsh, Amorn Watanapong, and Jeff Woods.

I would like to also thank my dear friend and secretary, Joanne Inda, who continually took care of the small details as well as the large ones in order to make the production of this book come together smoothly. She has kindly given much extra time for its coordination and collation.

Acknowledgment is also given to George Post and Chris Witzke for the photography of Diana Kwan's work.

It is with much love that I acknowledge the continuous, cheerful encouragement and moral support given by my wife, Marlies. Her assistance, always there, was just what was needed to see this project through. Thanks once again, Marlies, as always.

Wayne Barton

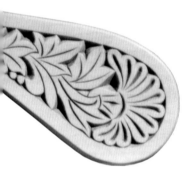

Chip Carving
as Art

Art is the soul of civilization. Without it every society would be a gray existence. History records that through the ages, even under the most depressed conditions, man turns to music, song, dance, and the tactile arts for self-expression and communication, even survival. We all have an innate ability and propensity to express ourselves artistically in one form or another. Fortunate are those who heed the inclination. It is a fulfillment in life like no other.

Traditions

In English it's called chip carving. In Germanic countries it's referred to as *Kerbschnitzen*, meaning notch or groove carving. Variations of this style of carving can be found in nearly every culture and time in history. Eastern European countries such as Poland, Ukraine, and Romania all have indigenous styles and traditions of chip carving. The Scandinavian countries also have a strong tradition of chip carving with styles peculiar to their area. France, Belgium, and Italy are not to be excluded. Certain areas of these countries also have strong chip-carving traditions.

While there are several reasons why chip carving has spread so widely, simplicity would be a major one. The tools used, the designs, and the actual carving process are all really quite simple. This puts the possibility to do chip carving within the reach of everyone. Indeed, at least since the Middle Ages (about A.D. 500 to 1500) it has been primarily the common man who performed and caused chip carving to proliferate.

Another reason would be chip carving's decorative and functional nature. It appeals to those who enjoy lending their own artistic expression to ordinary objects. Unlike other forms of carving, chip carving is nearly always applied to items already in a finished state, such as boxes, plates, chairs, spoons, etc.

Styles of Chip Carving

Today, chip carving is much expanded from its humble beginnings. Generally, its designs can be distinguished in three separate categories: these are geometric, freeform, and positive imaging. Often these different classifications are combined, increasing the visual complexity, diversity, and interest of the finished piece.

Traditional Geometric Designs

Geometric designs are exactly what their name implies. Using a ruler and compass, basic geometric shapes such as the circle, square, diamond, rectangle, etc., are put together in any number of ways to create what might be considered a traditional pattern that is normally incised into the wood. This harkens back to the original roots of chip carving. Examples of geometric designs can be found as far back as those decorating biblical artifacts and even earlier.

Free-Form Motifs

Free-form design takes any form for its subject. Flowers and birds are frequently used, but other items such as a ship or a shoe are just as correctly used. In free-form, the subject may be outlined with a simple incised groove or more elaborately carved by defining the individual parts of a subject, such as carving the individual feathers of a bird.

Positive image carving in progress.

Positive Imaging

Positive imaging is a refinement and expansion of chip-carving design possibilities. Rather than incising a design into the wood, it removes the wood around a subject, effecting a relief carving using chip-carving techniques. This style is particularly successful in creating foliage, floral, and other organic patterns but certainly is not limited to these.

Because many of the artists whose work appears here carve in more than one style or elements thereof, it is difficult to present their work in one particular category. However, the reader will be able to distinguish one style from the other and when they are being used within the same carving. I feel that the carvings of each artist are best shown by displaying them together so that the particular artist's style and/or flair can be readily observed.

 # Resurgence of Chip Carving

With the reemergence and recognition of chip carving in recent years as the art form it truly is, a growing interest in its design has naturally followed. The assumption often is made that one must be "gifted" to be artistic. Stated another way, either you're born with talent or you're not. True, in every discipline of the arts there will be a few who rise above the general field and are regarded as extraordinary. But this does not preclude the rest of the population from being able to produce truly artistic work.

The forest would be very silent if no birds sang except the best. The mechanical skills of chip carving are easily learned, just by carving. The visual skills needed to create designs are acquired through observation and application. By studying the patterns and becoming familiar with the wide range of work being done by the artists presented in this book, you will soon develop the visual skills necessary to develop designs of your own.

My years of instructing others have demonstrated to me that with a little practice and understanding of the process, anyone can learn to carve wood. This is amply illustrated by the photos included herein.

Reviving Traditions & Forging New Directions

The exciting aspect of all this is that by adding her or his own vision, skills, and talent to virtually the same information and instruction, each carver has created work that is distinctly original.

Their collective work spans a broad spectrum of diversity from the simple to the complex; from the straightforward geo-

metric to the very imaginative positive imaging. It is a marvelous display of chip carving rich in design possibilities and superbly executed on a wide selection of objects.

This is a book easily studied. It is also hoped that it will encourage those who are inspired to try chip carving and fan the artistic flame that burns within each one of us.

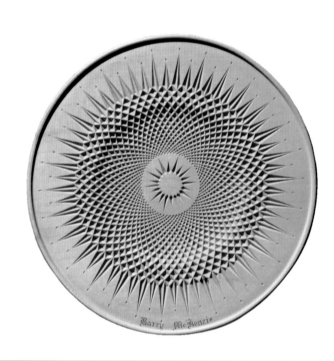

Tools & Materials

For centuries chip carving has been performed with quite a variety of cutting implements, including knives, gouges, chisels, and even razor blades. Often they were homemade and sometimes adapted from other tools. Many proved not to be as effective as desired for chip carving, and some were outright dangerous. In addition, as in other human endeavors, the beginner and unschooled student tends to surround himself with more tools than needed, erroneously assuming that he will make up in numbers what he lacks in skill and confidence.

Tools

One of the unexpected pleasures of the chip-carving style illustrated herein is the discovery of the limited number of tools and materials needed to do truly fine carving. And, unlike some other forms of carving, acquiring additional tools will not increase your skill or produce a better finished product.

Premier Chip-Carving Knives

The carvings in this book were predominantly executed with only two knives. They are the WB Premier chip-carving No. 1 cutting knife and the WB Premier No. 2 stab knife. Their design is the result of feedback I have received from my students over many years of teaching. I feel these tools offer improvements over those most used for years and others available today for several reasons.

One reason is that the blades are high-carbon true tool steel. Another is the greater downward angle of the No. 1 cutting knife. The tip of this blade is also more sharply pointed, allowing the carver to make curved cuts more easily as well as execute tighter corners and niches. The No. 2 stab knife has a longer blade edge, allowing longer "stabs" to be made, increasing design possibilities.

Another significant advantage of these knives is their ergonomically designed handles. The handles have been shaped from domestic wood and highly polished, allowing for a good grip and hours of comfortable, easy, nonfatiguing carving. A more satisfying handle will be hard to find. Since you're going to use only two knives, give yourself every advantage. Cheap, inade

Chip-carving knives designed by the Wayne Barton:
(Top) WB Premier stab knife; (Bottom) WB Premier cutting knife.

quate tools produce only disappointing results, and often are a waste of time and money.

The WB Premier No. 1 cutting knife is used to remove all wood chips. The WB Premier No. 2 stab knife is used to decorate and complement the work done by the cutting knife. The stab knife removes no wood at all; instead it cuts and spreads the wood, making permanent indented impressions of any variety of lengths, combinations, and designs. Although most work is done with the cutting knife, it is a mistake to disregard the capabilities of the stab knife. Students who neglect the stab knife deny themselves the full possibilities of chip carving. Likewise, an instructor who does not educate his students in the proper use and functions of the stab knife performs a great disservice.

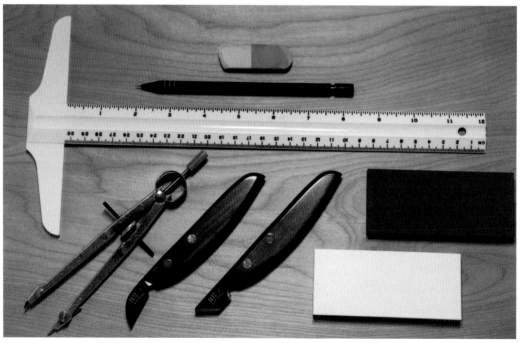

Tools needed for chip carving: T-square, pencil, cutting and stab Premier chip carving knives, draftsman's compass, eraser, and ceramic sharpening and polishing stones.

Other Tools

The remainder of the tools needed for chip carving are a pencil (a mechanical one with a 0.05 lead size works well), ruler, eraser, and drafting-type compass. Use a grade "B" lead for both the compass and pencil. This softer-grade lead makes legible lines without impressing the wood, and it is easier to clean off than the harder grades of lead. When it is time to clean all the excess pencil marks off your carving, you'll find that an ink eraser does it quickly and neatly.

Safety

With quality tools and their proper use, chip carving should be a safe and satisfying carving experience. Use common sense and develop a good set of guidelines to adhere to in your workshop.

Although you may have a table or workbench upon which to set your tools or your work, chip carving is best done with the maximum amount of control and leverage, which means doing all of your work in your lap. With your elbows close to your body, you will have added leverage and strength from your shoulders. Unless the workpiece is too large to hold, sitting at a table or workbench forfeits your leverage and strength.

Keep a clean workshop. Clean your chips as you carve. Don't leave little bits of wood in the bottom of your cuts. Keep your work clean and crisp.

Keep your tools sharp.

Holding your knives may seem awkward at first, but with practice they will become quite natural to you.

Make all cuts only as deep as is necessary to remove a chip. Ideally, you only make a cut once. In the case of larger chips, it may be advantageous to first remove the top half of the chip, and then go back to get the rest. A too-deep cut may split your workpiece, if the pressure is not relieved in this way. Never try using the cutting knife without some part of your hand or finger touching the work as a guide—or you will have no control.

Sharpening

The lack of a sharp edge to your tools can deprive you of the joy of carving. There are three criteria to the process of sharpening: sharpening at the correct angle, producing a sharp cutting edge, and producing a blade that is polished.

Chip carving, unlike all other forms of carving, which are executed by shaving wood, calls for the carver to insert the blade into the wood to remove specific shapes, pieces, or chips. The angle at which the blade is sharpened is critical but not impossible to achieve.

Flat ceramic sharpening stones (not rods) are best. They are so hard that even with extended use they remain flat. Unlike natural stones, the high quality of the ceramic stone is uniform and constant. Further, the ceramic stone requires no oil or water as lubricant in the sharpening process.

You need both a medium-grade and an ultra-fine stone. The angle of the properly sharpened edge is approximately 10 degrees or less. You can gauge the maximum angle by raising the knife off the stone just until a dime (U.S. 10-cent coin) can be slipped under the back edge of the blade. In many cases you will want an angle less than this.

Sharpen the cutting knife first on the medium-grade stone, keeping equal pressure on the heel and tip of the blade. A back-and-forth movement with pressure on one side, and then equally of the other side, works well. This method should sharpen the blade without a heavy burr. Check light

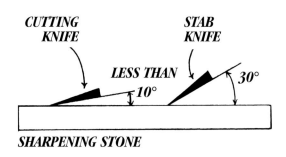

Angles for sharpening cutting and stab knives.

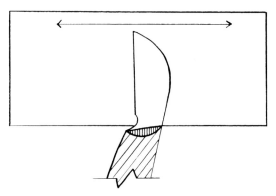

Slide the knife blade back and forth across the stone to sharpen.

reflection by holding the knife under a bright light with your finger on the tip, to cut any glare. When there is no burr and you should be able to see no light reflecting off the edge, then you are ready for polishing.

Use the ultra-fine ceramic stone to hone each side equally so that you don't create a burr. Polishing the metal in this way will assure that the blade will glide easily through the wood rather than drag.

Check for light reflection again, and cut diagonally across the grain of a piece of scrap wood to check for drag. Your knife should flow smoothly and steadily.

The stab knife is sharpened with the same stones and procedures used for the cutting knife, with the exception of the sharpening angle. The angle for the stab knife is approximately 30 degrees. Because the stab knife is used only for impressing or indenting the wood to enhance a design, the angle of the cutting edge is more crucial than its sharpness.

The frequency of sharpening will depend on the quality of the steel in your blades, the variety of wood being used, and the type of cuts being made. Some kinds of wood can dull a blade quickly, and deep and curved cuts can wear an edge in no time. You will develop a feel for when it is time to hone your blades on the ultra-fine stone. You will find yourself using more pressure to get the same results than you did initially. Also, you will notice that light begins to reflect from the edge as it dulls.

Selection of Wood

Not all types of wood can be used effectively for chip carving, and some are better than others. There are several criteria to consider in selecting wood for carving.

Degree of Hardness

Unlike carving with a chisel, chip carving with the proper knives is done with one hand without the aid of a mallet. Softer woods thus allow a greater degree of control to the carver. Less pressure while carving permits you to concentrate on applying smooth, flowing cuts to your design. Wood that is too soft will crush or tear under a sharp knife. Certain applications such as furniture or a cutting board may require a harder wood.

Natural Beauty & Color

Select your wood with an eye toward its color and beauty. Light-colored woods give a better contrast of shadow and light than dark-colored woods. However, if your carving is to make a muted statement in the overall work, as with some furniture, then the tendency of dark or stained woods to obscure the light/shadow effect may be what you want.

Suggested Woods

All of the carvings shown in the book are executed in basswood, butternut, eastern white pine, and walnut. These woods, particularly basswood (also referred to as linden or lime), are exceptionally well suited for chip carving, although they are not the only ones that carve well. Jelutong, catalpa, buckeye, tupelo, cypress, mahogany, and black willow can also be used.

Basswood is an easy and satisfying wood to carve. It is pale cream to yellowish brown with a uniform fine texture. Basswood is essentially identical to what Europeans know as linden/lime. Linden is a family of trees—*Tiliaceae*—of which the genus *Tilia* is generally termed linden, native in temperate regions. The North American linden is commonly referred to as "basswood" or "whitewood." This close-grained wood is most satisfying for any chip-carving project.

Quality and Pattern of Grain

"The tighter and straighter the grain the better" is a general guide for chip carving. Open-grain woods such as mahogany have a tendency to split and limit the intricacy of the design. Irregularly grained woods lessen your control of the cut, making accuracy more difficult. Spectacular or exotic grained wood tends to work against you. Unspectacular, straight-grained wood is most satisfying.

Butternut is a hardwood sometimes also called white walnut. The heartwood is a light brown, frequently with pinkish tones or darker brown streaks. It is moderately light in weight (about the same as eastern white pine), rather coarse-textured, and moderately soft. It resembles black walnut, especially when stained.

Eastern white pine is sometimes confused with Ponderosa pine and western white, and also known in some areas as Weymouth pine as well as by other names. This is a straight-grained, even-textured softwood that is good for chip carving. The heartwood is light brown, often with a reddish tinge; exposure to air darkens the wood. Eastern white pine is inexpensive yet easy to work, and takes a polish well.

Black walnut can have a beautiful color that makes it desirable to work with. The heartwood varies from light to dark brown. Black walnut is normally straight-grained and easily worked with tools. It is a dense wood that can hold detailed carving.

A great many woods are suitable for chip carving. You may prefer to use a regional wood that you can easily obtain locally rather than seeking out more exotic woods like mahogany, the harvesting of which may be endangering its existence or that of an entire forested region. As well, it is useful to be aware that some woods that are beautiful to cut and carve, such as the softwood, common or European yew, can be toxic, especially in the form of sawdust.

The tools and materials recommended and shown in this book, including the basswood plates and boxes, are generally available from most woodcarving suppliers.

Should you have difficulty finding them, however, contact the author for some specific suppliers.

Wayne Barton
The Alpine School of Woodcarving, Ltd.
225 Vine Avenue
Park Ridge, IL 60068
847-692-2822 or
fax 847-692-6626

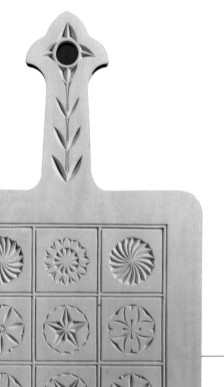

The Process

Seeing a chip-carving project through from start to finish is more than the mere application of a select number of techniques and stock patterns. The woodcarver's genius is to visualize a completed work and then hold that vision ever constant as the carver physically recreates what is already seen in the mind's eye.

Conceiving a Project

In conceiving any chip carving, it is usually a border that sets the tone or feel of the carving. It may be a single line or intricate enough to render the carving complete. Another little-remarked aspect of chip carving involves taking the basic geometrical shape of the workpiece, such as a square or rectangle, and transforming it into a decorative piece through what is called sculpted edges. By cutting any combination of notches and scoops in the edges of the wood, you can give the piece the appearance of taking on another form or shape.

One of the most traditional aspects of conceiving a chip carving is the incorporation of rosettes and grids. The design possibilities are endless. A completed carving of a rosette can appear daunting in its com-

plexity, but when seen as a simple line drawing, it can be more readily understood.

Free-form motifs, such as those found in Switzerland, can be things with which the carver may be familiar in his everyday life. Motifs include flowers, birds, and nearly any natural form, many of which have symbolic significance. Free-form motifs can be representational, stylized, or abstract.

Where curved lines are drawn, making crescent-shaped chips will add a fullness or three-dimensional appearance to a carving, especially for free-form designs.

Vary and combine geometrical shapes in a carving for a look of life and vitality. Using the same type and size chip (particularly the three-cornered chip) may be executed mechanically correctly, but often renders a piece artistically dull.

In conceiving the chip-carving project, it is not so much the importance of the individual element as it stands alone, but rather how you, as artist, visualize the completed work, combining each element into a unified, self-expressive whole. You will need technical mastery, precise layout, and crisp execution, but it is the imagination and conception of the whole that you bring to the uncarved piece that ultimately distinguishes your art.

Marking Out

It is best to draw your design directly on the wood. All lines that can be drawn with a straightedge or compass should be done this way. Because most pieces vary in size, drawing directly on the wood will allow you to proportion your work accurately. In some cases, it will be easier to space free-form designs properly on a piece or within a larger design if you trace them from a pre-drawn sketch.

When tracing, use graphite paper, which cleans off wood like an ordinary pencil. Regular carbon paper is greasy and difficult to remove. For easy final cleaning of pencil and tracing marks, use an ink eraser.

If your workpiece is absolutely flat—no scallops, no raised border or dishing—there is an easy way to transfer any single-line drawing, or pattern, to wood: simply making a photocopy of it, placing the copy facedown on the wood, and ironing it. Cleaning or removing the ironed-on pattern lines, however, is a bit more difficult than removing relatively clean pencil lines. It is advantageous to be careful to carve all of the line off when executing the design. Also be aware that this makes a "mirror image" of the pattern. To get a right-side-up transfer, such as for lettering, first make a transparency. Then copy the transparency backwards on regular paper. When you place the paper facedown on the wood, this time the lettering, or pattern, will come out correctly.

Cutting Positions & Handling Techniques

To carve effectively, you need to be comfortable with how to use your knives. There are two positions for the cutting knife. For the first position, hold the knife in your right hand and place the first joint of your thumb (curved outwards) at the end of the handle by the blade on the lower inside ridge of the handle. Wrap the rest of your fingers around the handle. (Left handed carvers, like the author, simply reverse this process.) Your thumb and your knuckles should rest on your work, guiding and supporting the blade as though it were a sixth digit. Your thumb should never leave the handle while you are cutting, as it might when peeling potatoes.

The second position is achieved by moving the thumb directly on top of the spine of the handle with the first knuckle of the thumb still next to the blade, not on it.

The stab knife is held with one or two hands perpendicular to your work. It is thrust downward to make an impression along the length of its indentation to the desired depth.

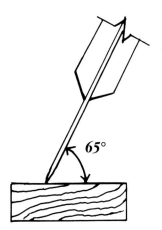

The No. 1 cutting knife is properly inserted in the wood at a 65-degree angle.

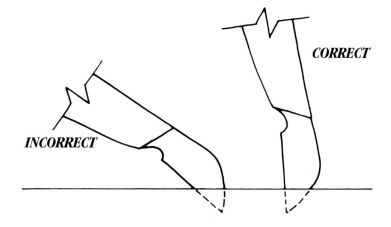

When you are making curved cuts, stand the knife perpendicular to the wood rather than at a low angle..

Carving

The two holding positions for the cutting knife give you the proper (and same) angle for carving in opposing directions. Held properly and consistently, your blade will always be in the wood at the correct angle.

The first position is used for all line cuts, both straight and curved. It is also used for the first and third cuts of small, regular, triangular chips. When using the first position, turn your wrist away from your body.

The second position is used only for the second cut of the same triangular chips. You will have much more control if, when you are making line cuts or larger curved chips in the first position, you simply keep turning your work in your lap rather than keep changing positions.

To carve straight lines successfully, train your eye always to look ahead of the blade. Never look at the blade itself and don't use a straightedge as a guide. In a short time, you will be making straight lines more quickly than you imagined possible.

For good contrast of light and shadow, make your cuts or chips at a 65-degree angle in the wood. When making curved cuts, stand the knife up. The tighter or smaller the curve, the more perpendicular the knife must be to the carving. It is impossible to drag an excess amount of metal around a curve without producing a chatter or choppy appearance. However, the 65-degree angle at which the blade is inserted into the wood to scribe the wall of the chip does not change.

When two tapered chips of the same shape must be brought to a single point, you will be able to keep the center ridge straight and unbroken if you bring only one chip all the way to the center and hold the second back slightly. This is especially true when cutting across the grain.

Don't over-carve a piece. In most cases, the area you leave uncarved is as important as what you do carve.

▦ Finishing

Remove the pencil or graphite paper marks from your carving with an ink eraser. Marks left on carved ridges should be erased only with great care, because they may be delicate and could break off if handled roughly. With all marks removed, lightly sand the work with 220-grit sandpaper, This will freshen the entire surface and prepare it for finishing.

Finishing wood is an art in itself, in which I am not an expert. But what I do know comes from years of trial and error as well as from the teaching of my father, who was an expert. Whatever method you choose to use, I do recommend that you finish your carvings—not least to protect them from fingerprints and dirt accumulating over time. Once finished, you will be able to dust and clean the surface without harming the wood.

Polyurethane or lacquer (usually dull, sometimes satin, rarely gloss) can be used to achieve an excellent natural finish. Apply finish by spray rather than brush. Brushing tends to fill in the carved areas, detracting from the smooth, crisp appearance. Three thin coats will do nicely. Allow each application to dry thoroughly, sanding lightly between coats with 220-grit sandpaper. Do not sand after the last coat is applied.

If you choose to stain your carving, be aware that softer woods, such as those typically used for chip carving, take more color in exposed grain. Always test-stain a piece of scrap wood that is the same type as the carving. I prefer gel stains to oil stains, because the oil stains penetrate too deeply. A light sealer coat of polyurethane, lacquer, etc. before staining is a good idea since it seals the surface more than the cuts, allowing the stain to accentuate the carving. The sealer will also raise any of the fuzzy surface grain, enabling you to sand the surface, not the cuts, with the 220-grit sandpaper.

Work one side of the piece at a time. Brush the gel over the surface, working it thoroughly into the cuts and grooves as you go. Cover a side completely, but don't apply the gel excessively. Use a clean, lint-free cloth to wipe off the excess gel. With a small, clean brush, work the excess out of the cuts. Keep wiping and cleaning your brush as you go.

Repeat for the remaining sides. Then let the piece dry thoroughly.

Continue just as with applying the natural finish. Spray three thin, even coats of polyurethane (or any other finish you prefer). Be sure the surface is dust-free before each spraying, and be careful not to sand through the stain. Always spray in a well-ventilated area.

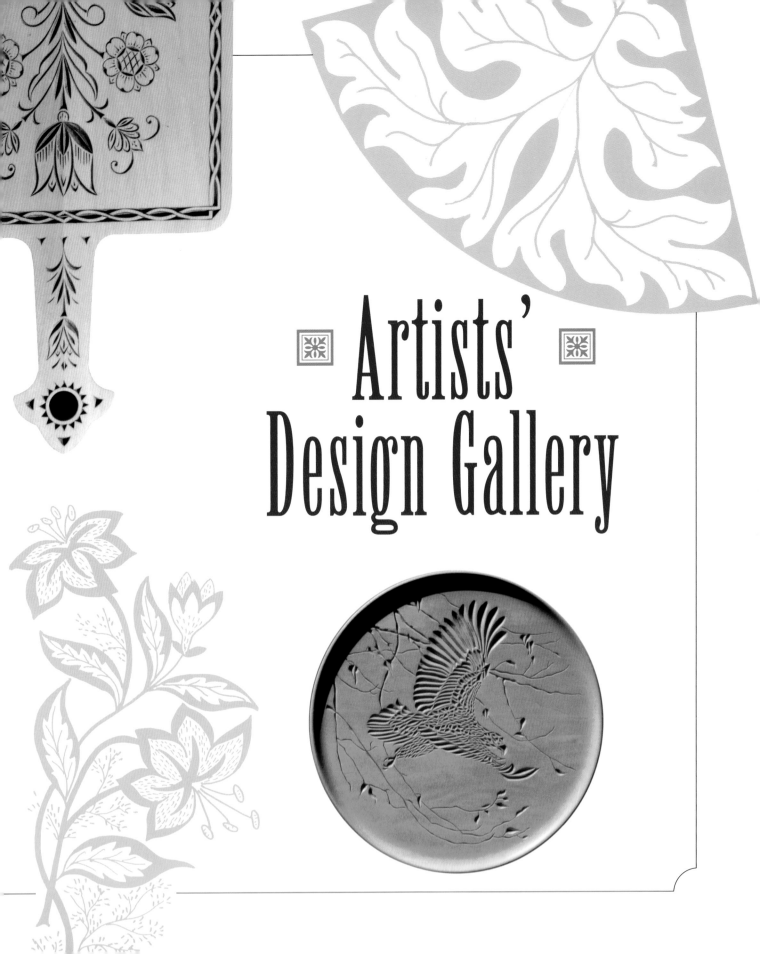

Artists' Design Gallery

Charles Baker

JOLIET, ILLINOIS

Chuck retired in 1991 after 32 years of teaching high school business education. He divides his time between his homes in Illinois and Florida. He has taken up carving since his retirement and devoted much of his spare time to this hobby. As a hobbyist, Chuck prefers to carve a variety of different subjects and constantly searches for new applications of his designs.

Basswood lamp base.

Advent candleholder.

Line-drawing detail of the design.

Timothy J. Balda

LORAIN, OHIO

Tim used his MBA as a real estate developer and builder for several years. He presently is a full-time woodcarver and owns Woodworks, Ltd., a mail-order supplier of specialty kits and woodcarving supplies. He also teaches woodcarving locally. Accuracy is the keynote of his design and execution, which include a wide variety of subject matter.

Spanish galleon on a 20-inch plaque.

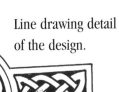

Line drawing detail
of the design.

14-inch basswood
Celtic cross.

Candlestick holder
with Celtic tree-of-life design.

18-inch basswood cross.

14-inch rim
basswood plate.

16-inch basswood disk.

Windswept tree
on an 8-inch
disk.

David W. Crothers

HATBORO, PENNSYLVANIA

David is a labor relations negotiator and mediator for the U.S. government. He principally combines his love of classical music and interest in quality music boxes for his area of carving. He custom-builds and designs all of his work, making each piece he produces a very special one-of-a-kind work of art. His is a very lyrical approach to design, strongly influenced by music, meticulously and flawlessly executed.

Music box lid.

Music box lid.

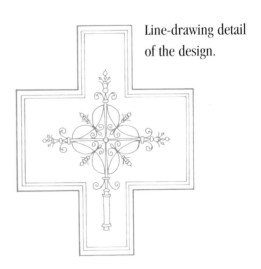

Line-drawing detail
of the design.

Rosette and motto of J.S. Bach
written on all of his scores.

14-inch scalloped basswood plate.

Music box lid.

14-inch scalloped
basswood plate.

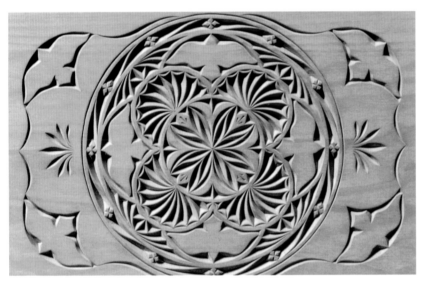

Basswood panel
on a jewelry box.

Donald A. Ecker

EXETER, ONTARIO, CANADA

Don is a semi-retired family physician whose hobbies include horses, airplanes, and woodworking. He has been chip carving for about eight years and uses his carving skills to decorate a variety of objects. His wife, Melva, a quilter, provides him with many patterns that are adaptable to chip carving.

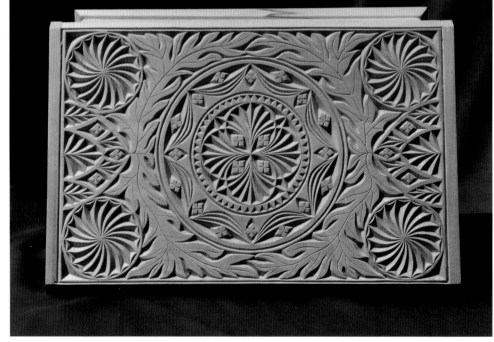

Basswood jewelry box lid, 9 x 14 inches.

Eight-inch octagonal basswood jewelry box.

Line-drawing detail of the design.

Two 12-inch double-beaded basswood plates.

Jeffrey J. Fleisher

HERNDON, VIRGINIA

Jeff has Master's Degrees in computer science and photographic science and instrumentation. This background gives him a keen eye for detail, proportion, and balance. Though Jeff has only been chip carving for about two years, his extraordinary skill and carving ability are evident.

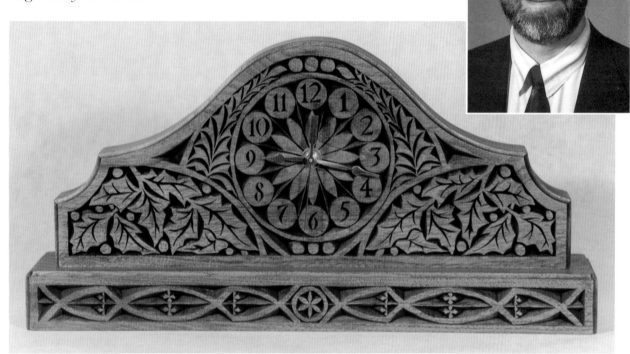

Basswood mantel clock.

Line-drawing detail of the design.

Englebert (Bert) Hirt

MILLBROOK, ONTARIO, CANADA

Bert was born and raised in Vienna, Austria, and emigrated to Canada in 1957. It was shortly thereafter that he included woodcarving to his many other interests. His carvings are very meticulously executed and strongly geometric. This is borne out by the numerous awards his carvings have received. Bert presently works in the nuclear industry as well as conducts his own business in woodcarving.

"Universe" design jewelry box lid, 10 x 15 inches.

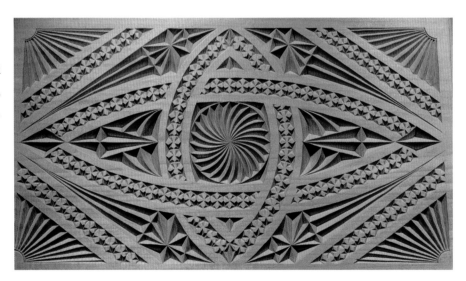

Eight-inch basswood bowl with lid.

Line-drawing detail
of the design,
about half size.

"Grand Jeté" wall hanging
on basswood board,
10 x 16 inches.

"Eye of the Storm" rosette
on basswood board,
8 x 10 inches.

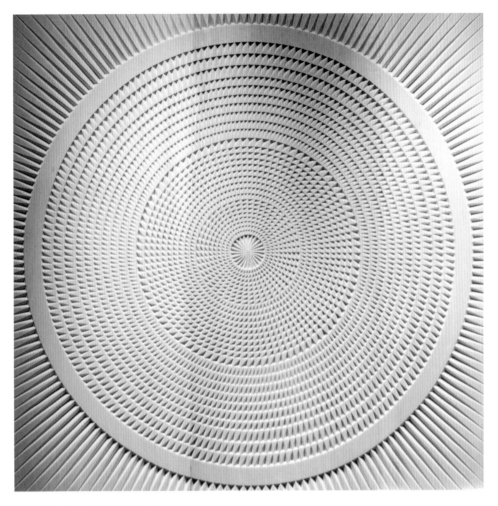

"Le Soleil II," 20 inches square.
This piece has a total of 3500 chips.

Mickey L. Hudspeth

DULUTH, GEORGIA

Mickey is Vice President of Sales of Wagner Communications, which designs and manufactures satellite communications products. For 30 years golf and woodworking have been his hobbies. About 12 years ago he became interested in carving and now combines this with his woodworking. Among his more popular pieces are his self-turned bowls and vases, often combining hardwood such as walnut with basswood and then carving the basswood. His pieces have been blue-ribbon winners throughout the southeastern states.

Coffee-table top.

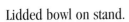

Lidded bowl on stand.

Line-drawing detail of the design.

Tabletop.

Bottom shelf
of the table.

Octagonal lidded container, basswood and walnut.

Pedestal bowl with lid, basswood and walnut.

Pedestal bowl with lid, basswood and walnut.

Sister Mary Julius

NASHVILLE, TENNESSEE

Sister Mary Julius is an o.p. Dominican Sister presently attached to the St. Cecilia Congregation in Nashville, Tennessee. She has performed several functions in connection with her order, including teaching, for many years. She has also acted as librarian. Presently she is the Registrar at St. Aquinus College. Although her daily obligations to her order require most of her time and devotion, she is still able to produce a large number of superbly artistic carvings. Her work is widely admired and duplicated by other carvers.

Line-drawing detail
of the design.

Butternut bookshelf end.

Three basswood serving trays, 16 1/2 x 18 inches.

Box lid, 4 x 14 inches.

Two box lids, 5 inches square.

Facial tissue box holder.

Box lid, 4 x 8 inches.

Triptych, 26 inches high.

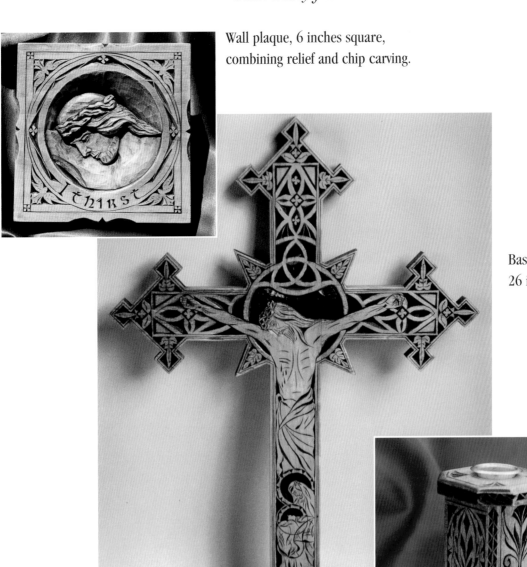

Wall plaque, 6 inches square, combining relief and chip carving.

Basswood crucifix, 26 inches high.

Basswood candlestick holder.

Larry Kampel

WELLSVILLE, PENNSYLVANIA

Larry is President of Kampel Enterprises, which manufactures a variety of products. For the past 50 years Larry has enjoyed a hobby of restoring and flying Stearman Bi-Planes. He is an innovative woodworker who also enjoys chip-carving the pieces he makes. The clock shown here is an original design in butternut. The roof shingles are carved into one board and not made individually. Larry uses the same emphasis of precision in his carving with which he does his woodworking.

Line-drawing details of the design.

Swiss chalet clock.

24-inch Swiss chalet standing clock.

Diana Kwan

SACRAMENTO, CALIFORNIA

Diana was born in Shanghai, China, and grew up in Hong Kong. She came to the United States to study microbiology at the University of California. Diana started carving in 1975 and developed a unique style that is strongly influenced by her heritage, combining chip and relief styles with painting. Her work is in the state capitol in Sacramento, California, and is highly prized in private collections.

"Chrysanthemum and Bamboo."

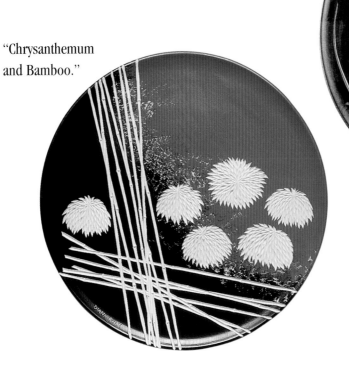

"Blossoms."

"Vase I."

Line-drawing detail of the design.

"Dancing."

"A Walk Through the Grass."

"African Tapestry."

"Rope Jacket."

"Chrysanthemum Kimono."

Barry G. McKenzie

LEBANON, MISSOURI

Barry took early retirement as a mechanical draftsman to devote his energies to full-time chip carving. He has adapted his drafting skills to execute very fine geometrical designs. Barry and his wife, Barbara, publish the "Chip Carving Newsletter" and operate a school for chip carving.

"Sunflower," 14-inch outside-beaded rim plate.

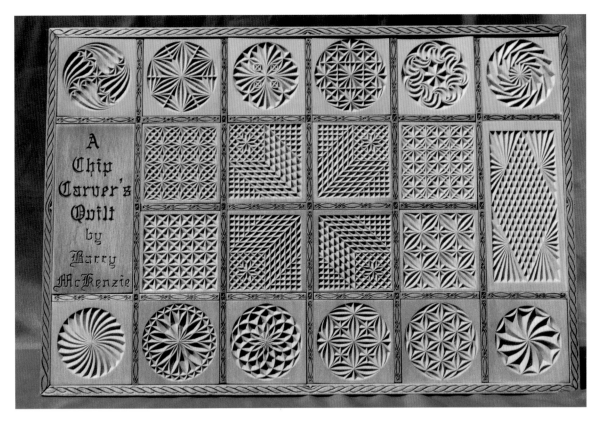

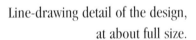

Chip-carved quilt, 15 x 22 inches.

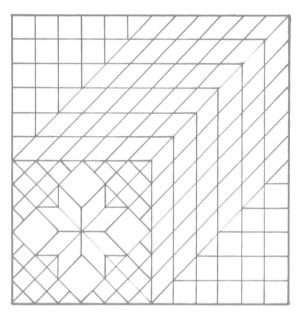

Line-drawing detail of the design,
at about full size.

Timothy Montzka

FOREST LAKE, MINNESOTA

Tim is a teacher by education and a plate-turner by trade, inheriting his interest in woodworking from his father and grandfather. His mother was the early inspiration for his chip carving. Among his many awards he has received the prestigious Gold Medal at Vesterheim, the Norwegian/American Museum in Decorah, Iowa.

14-inch rim basswood plate.

Basswood trunk lid, 20 x 27 inches.

Line-drawing detail
of the design.

Front panel of the trunk.

Bruce Nicholas

ST. PARIS, OHIO

Bruce works in sales and sales training in the industrial maintenance field. With his wife, Judy, Bruce also operates a woodworking and woodcarving business that offers products and carving lessons to the public. Together they continually explore and produce new products that are useful to the carving community and ways to carve them. Bruce emphasizes the need for continual study if one is to perfect his carving skills. This is a practice he strongly follows himself.

Hexagonal box lid.

Line drawing of the design,
about half size.

"Green Man" on plaque,
4 1/2 x 7 1/2 inches,
about three-quarter size.

Matchbox holder.

Candlestick box lid,
4 1/2 x 12 1/2 inches,
about half size.

Floral rosette on a 6-inch disk,
about half size.

Square, Prairie-style candlestick holder.

Karen Kolisch Oquin

ARVADA, COLORADO

Karen has been carving for approximately five years and emphasizes quality in her execution and design. She is active in craft shows, turning her hobby into a business. It is a sense of pride for her that her artwork is on display in many homes. Karen's carving shows a keen sense of proportion and balance in design.

Hawk in flight,
on 14-inch rim
basswood plate.

Line drawing detail of the design.

Christmas scene,
on 14-inch rim
basswood plate.

14-inch
scalloped rim
basswood plate.

Robert A. Ostmann

BETHESDA, MARYLAND

Bob has a private practice in patent law in additon to an engineering degree. He specializes in research of patent validity and infringement. Bob devotes as much time adapting and developing designs as he does carving, which is quite prodigious. Few carvers will ever produce the amount of fine work in both design and execution, whether they are hobbyists or professionals, that Bob does. His knowledge and understanding of contrast, proportion, balance, and chip carving in general are unequaled.

Jewelry box lid,
8 1/2 x 13 inches.

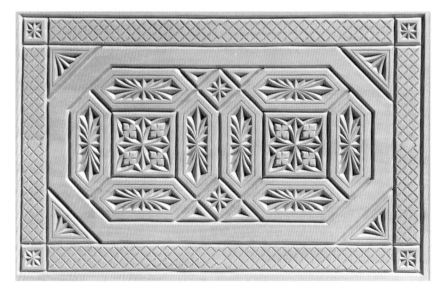

10-inch basswood scoop plate.

Line-drawing detail of the design.

Wall plaque, 8 x 12 inches.

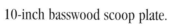

10-inch basswood scoop plate.

Standing clock, 8 1/2 x 12 inches, about half size.

10-inch basswood
scoop plate.

Coat hanger.

Barometer, 8 1/2 x 11 inches, about half size.

Swiss-style chair.

14-inch scalloped rim basswood plate.

10-inch basswood scoop plate.

Cookie jar,
8 1/2-inch diameter
x 10 inches.

10-inch rim basswood plate.

Wastebasket,
20 inches high.

14-inch basswood
scoop plate.

10-inch basswood
scoop plate.

12-inch rim
basswood plate.

12-inch scalloped,
beaded-rim
basswood plate.

Bread board, 8 x 15 inches.

Wall hangings, 3 x 12 inches.

12-inch rim basswood plate.

Eight-inch oval wall plaque.

Robert Rymark

ARLINGTON HEIGHTS, ILLINOIS

Bob retired after 30 years with a major utility company and now is a full-time cabinetmaker and woodcarver. He uses his wood-carving skills to enhance his unique woodworking and turnings. Bob is a strong promoter of chip carving and conducts classes aimed mainly at introducing non-carvers to chip carving.

12-inch bowl, basswood and walnut.

Basswood
jewelry box lid,
8 inches square.

Line drawing
of the design,
full size.

Lidded-pedestal bowl,
18-inch diameter,
basswood.

Six-inch-diameter basswood bowl.

Eight-inch outside-beaded,
flat basswood plate,
about half size.

Turned Christmas ornaments, basswood and walnut.

Robert E. Smith

FOLSOM, CALIFORNIA

Bob is a retired carpenter who has had an interest in woodcarving for nearly 20 years. In his early carving years he attended many classes and discovered that the style he enjoyed most was chip carving. His expertise is demonstrated by the numerous awards his carvings have received.

Jewelry box, basswood and walnut.

Black-capped heron, detail.

Line-drawing detail
of the design.

Black-capped heron and frame.

Detail of
picture frame.

Front panel of a jewelry box, basswood and walnut.

Picture frame,
detail.

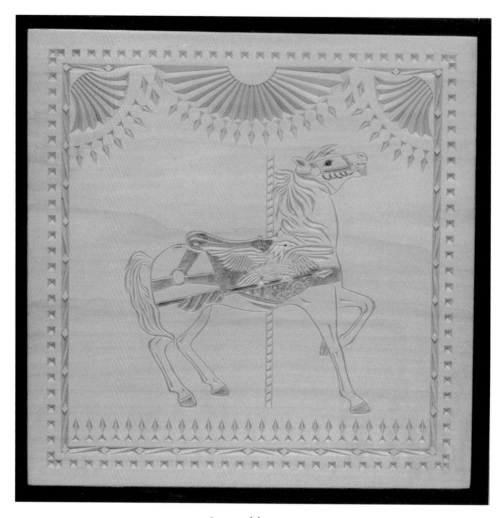

Carousel horse.

Margaret (Peggy) C. Walker

ETOBICOKE, ONTARIO, CANADA

Peggy is a retired professor of physical education and was also a women's intercollegiate basketball coach. She finished her career at McGill University. Having carved for several years, Peggy has a sharp artistic feel for balance and contrast. Her execution is precise and her designs are fresh.

12-inch octagonal
basswood plate.

Line-drawing detail of the design.

12-inch scalloped
basswood plate.

Basswood
candlestick
holders.

Mark Walsh

PIGEON FORGE, TENNESSEE

Mark is retired from a long, technically oriented career in sub-sea operations including military, commercial, and recreational diving. He is active in the Smoky Mountain Tennessee Valley School of Woodcarving. Sharing his knowledge of carving is a source of joy for him. Mark is constantly exploring new avenues of design to extend his talent.

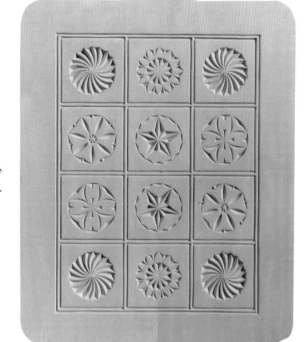

Basswood butter board,
9 x 14 inches.

Ruby-throated hummingbird and morning glory
on a 10-inch rim basswood plate.

Detail of hummingbird plate.

Butternut wall clock,
9 3/4 x 14 inches.

Line drawing of the design.

Cardinal and dogwood on a 12-inch scalloped basswood plate.

Chickadee and dogwood on a 12-inch-square scalloped basswood plate.

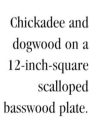

Amorn Watanapong

ELK GROVE VILLAGE, ILLINOIS

Amorn was born in Bangkok, Thailand. After finishing nursing school, she moved to the United States in 1974. Presently she is employed as a Registered Nurse. Her original designs, beautifully and delicately balanced, are strongly influenced by her ancestral heritage. Amorn is an artist who is not intimidated by large or difficult projects.

Tabletop.

Two side panels of a jewelry box,
5 1/2 x 7 1/2 inches,
about half size.

Tabletop.

Line drawing incorporating
motifs of the design.

Two side panels of a box,
7 1/2 x 9 inches,
about half size.

Tabletop.

Tabletop.

Two lamp bases, butternut.

Roses on box lid, 6 inches square, about half size.

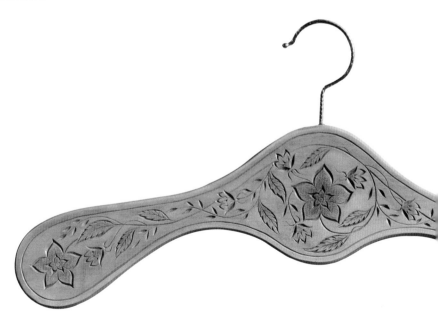

Coat hanger.

Detail of door panel, butternut.

Rev. Jeffrey Woods

CHICAGO, ILLINOIS

For the past eight years Jeff has served as the pastor of Immanuel Evangelical Covenant Church, an urban, multi-ethnic congregation. Prior to this appointment, he was a missionary to young people involved in the international drug culture in Afghanistan, India, Nepal, Amsterdam, and other major areas of Europe. He has been carving for five years and applies the same sensitivity to his carving as he does in his work with people.

Cross-in-heart motif on a 3 1/2-inch disk, full size.

Rose on a 5 1/2-inch oval, full size.

Line drawing of the design, full size.

Trefoil on a
4 1/2-inch disk,
about half size.

Basswood wall plaque,
10 1/2 x 18 inches.

Basswood coat hanger
on a 5 1/2-inch oval
with ship motif, about half size.

Jewelry box lid with lighthouse motif.

Cross and Star of David
tree ornament, 3 x 5 inches,
about three-quarter size.

Manger tree ornament.

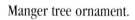

Floral design on a
3 1/2-inch disk,
about three-quarter size.

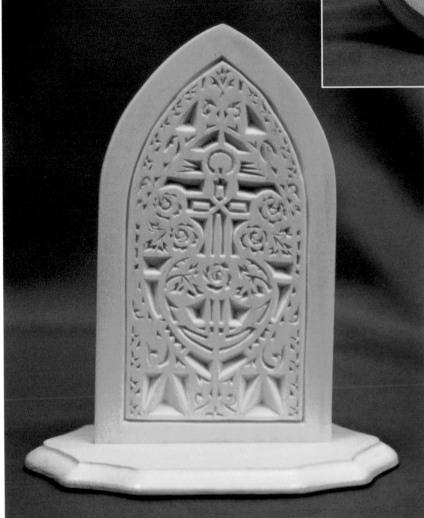

Gothic window motif,
3 1/4 x 6 inches,
about three-quarter
size.

About the Author

Wayne Barton is an American-born professional woodcarver who lives in Park Ridge, Illinois, with his Swiss wife, Marlies, and their children. First given an interest in woodcarving at the age of five by his Norwegian grandfather, he has had a serious interest in, and love for, carving all his life.

Mr. Barton took his formal training in Brienz, Switzerland, and his carvings can be found in private collections in Europe and North America. He is the Founder and Director of the Alpine School of Woodcarving, Ltd., and devotes much of his time to teaching throughout North America and in Switzerland.

Although versed in all disciplines of carving, he specializes in chip carving and has won both national and international awards and recognition for his work. Wayne Barton is recognized as the leading authority in the field of chip carving today.

Index